It's not often one of y(calls you with a work idea. I g ride BMX, and even as I drift. of mountain biking, he was always one of the gr... wanted to do some cartoons for Pinkbike, so it was a relief when his illustrated proposal was the best pitch deck I'd ever seen. Still is. It was an easy yes, and "Sunday Comics with Taj" was a hit in the mountain bike community.

I had the opportunity to see more of Taj's process when he visited during our annual Field Test. He'd always have a list of ideas in his notebook—plays on words, questions about why things are the way they are. Despite being one of the best BMXers on the planet, in many ways Taj is an outsider to the bike industry. He loves riding, but he's able to see the absurdity in the sport without being condescending or uninformed. That's one of the reasons people have connected with his work.

*Equal parts autobiographical introspection and self-deprecating witticism, **Back Before They Invented Open Face Helmets** is a remarkably poignant read. Some of the illustrations we originally commissioned have made their way into its pages alongside a collection of his other doodles. The book is incredibly funny, but it's also an inspirational roadmap for anyone trying something new. A beacon for staying motivated.*

 **Brian Park**
Head of Editorial at Pinkbike

Special thanks to Pinkbike, who paid me for some
of these comics. And, thanks to you, who bought
a book with a bunch of cartoons you could have
gotten for free on the internet.

First edition December, 2020

ISBN 978-0-578-79398-6

Published by Taj Mihelich
www.tajmihelich.com

BACK BEFORE THEY
INVENTED OPEN FACE HELMETS:

A BOOK OF CARTOONS AND DOODLES

BY TAJ MIHELICH

Contents

Originally for the Reynolds Family

Just Because I Think There Should Be Some Words Here

This is a mostly light hearted book of my dorky cartoons but I'm starting it off with a story that includes a terrible tragedy.

Chris Rye, of the *Props BMX Video Magazine* series that documented the goings on in BMX for most of my professional riding career, was on his way up to visit me. He was driving to my new small town home in the woods to interview me for a video project called "Life After Pro." The idea was to find out what direction I'd taken in life after hanging up my bike riding career. I wasn't sure how to answer that... I was still kind of struggling with it. What was life going to be after pro?

My first attempt at entering the "real world" was to just throw myself into my new job with the same single-minded focus that I'd had for bike riding. With no idea how to balance a healthy work life, I quickly overdid it.

For years I was a bike bum. I rode around on my bike for a living, and some days maybe I didn't feel like riding and so I didn't. I let my motivation flow naturally, and if it ever waned, I trusted that it would be back soon. And people would fly me around the world to wear their t-shirt in a bike comp. Maybe I'd feel like going off, or maybe I would decide to lay around in the hotel with a backache. I was used to doing whatever I wanted because bike riding was the only thing I wanted to do. I had a good run but it couldn't last forever.

A surgery, six blurry months of pain pills during a slow recovery, a healthy dose of good ol' natural aging (I was 37), and all of a sudden I was sitting at a desk in an office. I had a "job" and I went to "work." My little trick bike had been retired for a bike with a basket I could fit my dog into. It was an abrupt shock to my system. I worked at a dream job. I was surrounded by really great people (who have always been supportive and understanding) but it was so unlike the way the rest of my life had been.

Approaching office work the same way I approached riding—making it the focus of my life—didn't seem to satisfy me the way riding had. Riding had been everything to me and seemed fulfilling enough to be the only thing. Most importantly, riding had been a state of constant creativity. What new ideas could I imagine and bring to life? Often they were subtle, some slight deviation in a familiar line on a ramp, but there was always something new to learn or try. It was a part of my mind I couldn't turn off. I needed to find a new way to let it out.

With no conscious effort to do so, I started doodling. Any piece of paper that ended up in front of me (no matter how serious the office meeting) would end up covered with the unfocused creative juices leaking from my brain. I enjoyed drawing, and I would make myself laugh, but the doodles weren't anything I had ever put any value on.

I burned myself out at the office and decided the solution was to move to the woods in search of a quieter and more peaceful life (though I would still keep working for the office remotely). I'd always pictured my future self living somewhere with seasons, trees, and fresh air, so this seemed like the time to try it. However, I hadn't addressed the real problem. I was trying to fill the massive void left by my bike riding career with my new office job. No matter how hard I worked, I still felt a bit empty, yet stretched so thin there was no room in my life for anything else.

And so I decided that during the interview I would tell Chris Rye, "Unless you're Dave Mirra, life after pro can be a hard transition." Dave was one of the most talented and successful riders of all time and, like the *Props Video Magazines*, he was a fixture in BMX through my whole riding career. We were both pro at the same time and we were both about the same age. I would almost say we were peers, but I wouldn't want anyone to think I meant that we were equals. No one could claim to be equals with the mastery of Dave Mirra on a bike. How about guy-I-looked-up-to-who-I-thought-had-it-all-figured-out?

Dave's "Life After Pro" seemed to have it all. At least, that's how it looked to me through the peephole of Instagram. He seemed to be fit and healthy, had a nice family, and successfully moved on to other challenges with bigger wheels. Admittedly, I'd lost touch with him through the years. I unintentionally bailed on our friendship when I jumped ship on the road trip we started together with Joe Rich fifteen years before.

Dave picked us up in snowy Bethlehem, PA with some sketchy car he'd bought for a thousand dollars (I lived in B-Town for a year or so to be close to the legendary Posh trails). We traveled down the East Coast, stopped to ride occasionally, and laughed non-stop at Dave's jokes. I think we all rode a dirt contest at a BMX race on the way (a rare instance of Dave riding dirt) and visited an early version of the Greenville park. When we hit Austin, I just refused to get back in the car. I couldn't bear the idea of going back to the cold of Pennsylvania. It was a selfish move to abandon my road trip buddies at the halfway point and Dave and I talked very little after that.

I was thinking about that road trip from long ago, waiting for Chris Rye to show up, when terrible news arrived. Dave Mirra had killed himself. Saying the news "arrived" doesn't do the moment justice. Maybe "hit"? The news *hit* me like a tidal wave. *Bowled me right over* and left me feeling completely scrambled. Dave had been such an untouchable hero in BMX. Why did he do it? CTE was getting a lot of press at the time—did all his concussions contribute? What else was going on in his life? Was he also trying to find his way in *life after pro*? If Dave couldn't make it how could anyone? How could I?

Chris Rye took a bit over a year to finish up the video interview we did the next day. During that time I spent a lot of energy trying to imagine why Dave did it. Thinking about him demanded I make some changes in my own life. I reevaluated my mental health, for one. I spent some months with a therapist and started thinking about the trauma I'd put my brain through bouncing it off the ground for years. I enrolled in a CTE study to address my slipping memory. Watching Chris Rye's *Props* box set, I was able to document at least twenty-six times that I had been knocked solidly unconscious falling off my bike. I sat through hours of videos and would see myself rack up concussions that I had forgotten at events I didn't remember. For a while I got weekly cranial sacral massages that are supposed to help heal brain damage. They were a bit hippy-essential-oil-mumbo-jumbo but I can't deny that they helped. I stepped away from the office job that I had let stress me out so much (though I'm grateful to Fairdale Bikes for keeping me a part of things). I made a big effort to reduce stress across the board.

I rode my bikes without demanding that they become a means of self expression. In the winter, I cross-country skied slowly. Gliding around, looking at trees, and taking in the beauty of fresh, silent snow in the woods. And most importantly—at least in the sense of this book and why I've taken us into this sad story with a terrible tragedy—I decided to draw stuff for a living. I made this decision not because I was brilliant at it, and not because anyone was actually offering to pay me for it (yet), but because I laughed when I did it.

This is a collection of goofy and corny comics that made me laugh while drawing them. They're not, maybe, the best representations of how my drawing and painting skills have been growing… I've got a whole lot more progression to go before I'd consider putting out that book. This is all completely stress free "work." Just odd thoughts and doodles that came out whether I wanted them to or not. They're not encumbered with trying to be art or even bothered with being well-designed. My sincere hope is that you might maybe find a giggle in here somewhere.

They are presented for your entertainment… *hopefully.*

12 THINGS THAT PROBABLY SUCK ABOUT BEING BEST FRIENDS WITH AN ELEPHANT

1. NEVER ENDING TRUNK JOKES.

2. DOUBLES YOGA PHOTO SHOOTS.

3. ALWAYS WHISPERING INAPPROPRIATE THINGS INTO YOUR EAR WITH HIS TRUNK.

4. WILL DRINK YOUR MILKSHAKE.

5. IN KARATE CLASS, IT IS IMPOSSIBLE TO DEFEND AGAINST HIS QUADRUPLE-PRONG-OF-DEATH ATTACK.

6. MAKES FUN OF HOW LITTLE YOU CAN LIFT WITH YOUR NOSE.

7. ALWAYS PiCKS THE SAME RESTAURANT.

8. THE TRUNK JOKES, SERiOUSLY... THEY GET OLD, DUDE.

9. IT'S LIKE BEING FRIENDS WITH A LIVING SELFIE STICK.

10. EARS SMACK YOUR FACE DURING TANDEM BIKE RIDES.

11. ACTUALLY VERY DANGEROUS AT HEAVY
METAL SHOWS.

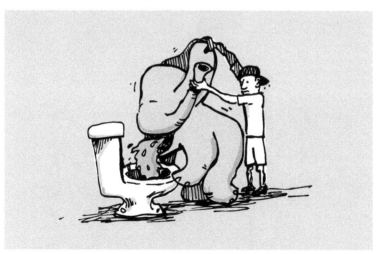

12. SUCH AN ORDEAL WHEN HE DRINKS TOO MUCH.

GREETiNGS GONE WRONG

A FRiEND APPROACHES, WHiCH OPTION DO YOU CHOOSE?

HANDSHAKE VS HiGHFiVE

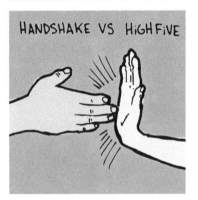

HANDSHAKE VS FiSTBUMP

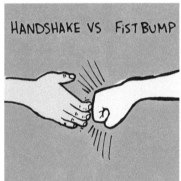

HANDSHAKE VS HUG

HANDSHAKE VS. VULCAN SALUTE

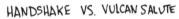
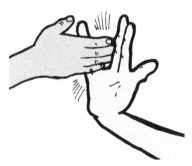

ALOHA SHAKA VS. BESOS
[KISSES]

LOW FIVE VS. HIGH FIVE

BUTTER FLY KISSES
VS. PINKY SHAKE

HUG VS. ELBOW BUMP

BOW VS. CHEST BUMP

TABLETOP TABLETOP

6 BMX TRICKS YOU PROBABLY SHOULDN'T DO

1. THRU THE HANDLEBAR BARHOP.

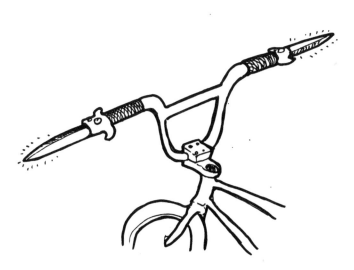

2. QUADRUPLE BARSPINS WITH SWITCHBLADE GRIPS.

3. LAKE JUMP WITH CEMENT BLOCKS TIED TO YOUR ANKLES.

4. ATTEMPT TO ESCAPE FROM A STRAIGHT-JACKET WHILE JUMPING THE MEGA RAMP®.

5. THIS GRIND.

6. WHATEVER THIS IS.

NOSE WHEELIE

Originally for Pinkbike

FAST PLANT

10 GOOD NOSE JOBS

1. DOG WALKER

2. CROSSING GUARD

3. SUSHI CHEF

4. RODEO RIDER

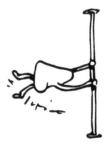

5. POLE DANCER

6. RAPPER

7. MOGUL SKIER

8. DolPHiN TRAiNER

9. PROFESSiONAL TRi-ATHlETE

10. MATTRESS TESTER

On the side of the road outside of town is this "D E ER SKULL BoiLiNG" sign. It is an attraction to out-of-towners who stop in wonder to take pictures. I never knew people boiled deer skulls before I moved up here, and I still have no idea why someone would want to. It's even more surprising to me that you could have a business solely focused on only one kind of skull. Do they turn away people who are hoping to have their gerbil or giraffe skulls boiled?

I thought about this sign so much that one night I decided to paint up a "professional" version. It was all fun and games until I showed up with my drill and some screws to hang the new sign without permission. It dawned on me that someone who makes their living boiling skulls might not have much of a sense of humor about it. My hands were shaking in fear as I hung my new sign over the old one.

For a few months, my sign stayed up and I continued to see tourists stopping to take pictures of it. One day it was just gone and I never heard another word about it.

THiNGS I SAW DURING A 15 MiNUTE ViSiT TO SENiOR DiSCOUNT DAY AT THE GROCERY STORE.

ON THiS DAY, THE LiNES PAiNTED ON THE PARKiNG LOT DiD NOT MATTER.

EVERY CART HAD A CANE OR A WALKER iN iT.

DROPPED PRODUCE STAYED DROPPED.

THE STORE'S MOBiLiTY SCOOTER WAS REVERSED iNTO THE PiNEAPPLES.

THERE WERE MANY LOW
SPEED CART COLLiSiONS.

BLOCKiNG THE ENTiRE AiSLE
AND NOT BEiNG ABLE TO HEAR
"EXCUSE ME" FROM BEHiND iS
JUST THE WAY iT iS.

A LOT OF CHECKS WERE
SLOWLY WRiTTEN AND MANY
PRiCES WERE CHALLENGED AT
THE REGiSTER.

SHOPPiNG CARTS, DEEMED TOO
DiFFiCULT TO RETURN, WERE LEFT TO
ROAM THE PARKiNG LOT FREELY.

THE FANTASTIC OlYMPIC SUCCESS (AND FAiluRE) OF MONTY THE NO ARMED DOG.

THERE'S SOMETHING ABOUT
BALANCING ON TWO WHEELS.

Monty

WHEN CORGIS ATTACK

7 THINGS THAT PROBABLY SUCK ABOUT BEING A GIRAFFE

1. THE KINK IN YOUR NECK FROM SLEEPING IN A HOTEL BED.

2. EVERYONE KNOWS IT'S YOU IN THE BATHROOM STALL.

3. IT TAKES FOREVER TO KNIT A TURTLENECK.

4. LOSING ALL YOUR FRIENDS TO CEILING FANS.

5. HOW STUPID THE WINDSCREEN LOOKS ON
YOUR MOTORCYCLE.

6. THOSE DAYS WHEN YOU CAN'T HAVE THE SUNROOF OPEN.

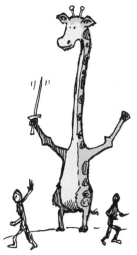

7. NO ONE iS iMPRESSED BY YOUR SWORD SWALLOWiNG ACT.

Together

We're all floating around on the same little rock together.

All of us, drifting through space with the bones of those who came before.

Technically speaking, there are a few astronauts orbiting in a space station who are not on the earth, but they all come home to universally report the same thing.

"We're all floating around on the same little rock... together."

Together

Together

Before corgis
were convinced to
be house pets...

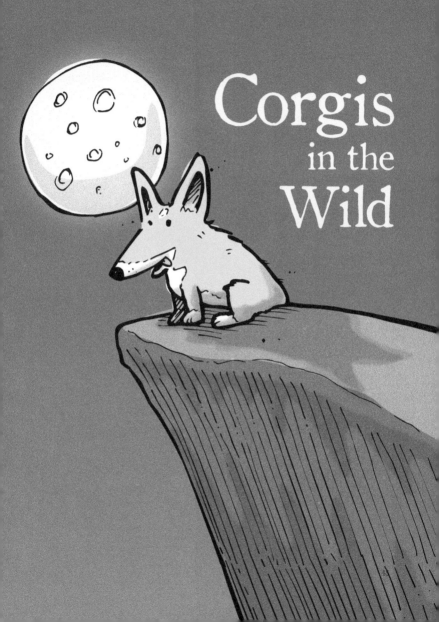

Corgis
in the
Wild

Corgis in the Wild

They traveled in packs with their
smaller cousins the Guinea Pigs and
the Hamsters.

46

They wandered the wilderness
in search of their favorite treats:
cat turds.

They napped often and wherever they
pleased.

And they hoarded vast treasures of squeaky toys.

The end... for now.

INTERNAL BATTLES

WHY DO WE HAVE TO FIGHT?

IT ALWAYS WORKS OUT
BETTER WHEN I STEER.

DROP iN
OR
DROP OUT

"YOU WEAR YOUR HEART ON YOUR SLEEVE,
AND I'LL WEAR YOUR SLEEVE ON MY HEAD."

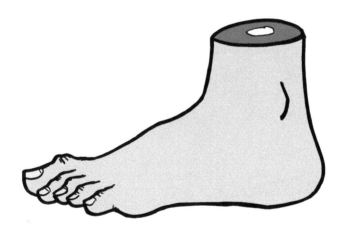

SOME DAYS JUST STAYING UPRIGHT IS A FEAT.

8 THINGS YOU PROBABLY SHOULDN'T DO IN THE TOUR DE FRANCE

1. STEAL PETER SAGAN'S FRONT WHEEL WHILE HE'S DOING WHEELIES FOR THE CAMERA.

2. RIDE WITH REALLY WIDE HANDLEBARS.

3. TRY TO GET THE ROOKIES TO FALL FOR THE OLD "SMELL MY CHAMOIS PAD" JOKE.

4. INVENT AN EVEN MORE DANGEROUS SUPERTUCK.

5. ORGANIZE ALL THE RIDERS TO SPELL WORDS DURING THE HELICOPTER SHOTS.

6. HELP THE RACE LEADER POOP MID-RACE WITHOUT STOPPING.

7. SQUiRT YOUR WATER BOTTLE SO EVERYONE THiNKS YOU'RE PEEiNG.

8. WHEN THE RiDER iN FRONT OF YOU STANDS UP, ADJUST THEiR SADDLE ANGLE.

BMX IN THE OLYMPICS

63

ARRRR BMX

LEGENDS of BMX

CHRIS MOLAR

MAT HOFFMAN

WOODY ITSON

DAVE FRYMOUTH

FUZZY HALL

CHRIS DOILY

COREY BOWHAND

VAN HOMAN

ROOFTOP

Originally for Dave Nourie

BLYTHER, WiLKERSON, HOFFMAN, & NOURiE

Come n' Shave It

BROKE MY ARM. THEY SENT ME TO SEE AN ORTHOPEDIC SURGEON.

I DECIDED TO GET A 2ND OPINION FROM THE INTERNET.

THEY PUT ME iN A CAST PAST THE ELBOW.

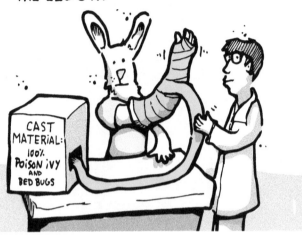

I HAD A DRAWING DUE THE NEXT DAY. IT WAS VERY DiFFiCULT SiNCE I COULDN'T USE MY DRAWING HAND.

NORMAL THINGS WERE A
SUPRISING CHALLENGE WITH MY
NON-DOMINATE HAND.

AFTER A WEEK THE CAST
STARTED TO GET VERY ITCHY...

...AND EXTREMELY STiNKY.

8 WEEKS LATER I WAS BACK TO NORMAL.

Originally for Pinkbike

PEOPLE WHO LIVE IN SCREEN HOUSES
SHOULDN'T THROW STONES EITHER.

15 *Important* Safety Tips For Mountain Bikers

1. KEEP YOUR LEGS AND ARMS BENT.

Originally for Pinkbike

2. KNOW YOUR ABILITY AND DON'T RIDE OVER YOUR HEAD.

3. CHOOSE YOUR LINE CAREFULLY.

4. WEAR KNEE PADS.

5. STAY HYDRATED.

6. STAY LOOSE.

7. KEEP YOUR EYES DOWN TRAIL.

8. FOCUS ON WHAT'S AHEAD.

HEAD PART

NON-HEAD
PART

9. PAY ATTENTION TO TRAIL SIGNS.

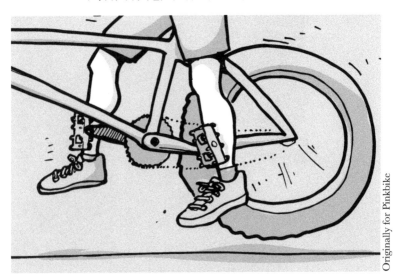

10. DO NOT LAND LIKE THIS.

Originally for Pinkbike

11. DO NOT OVER-PRESSURIZE YOUR DROPPER POST.

12. ALWAYS WEAR A HELMET.

13. DO NOT DO THIS TRICK ON PURPOSE.

14. MAKE SURE YOU HAVE A COMFORTABLE SADDLE.

Originally for Pinkbike

Originally for Pinkbike

15. WHEN GOING REALLY FAST ON A NEW BIKE ALWAYS
REMEMBER THIS: DEPENDING ON WHAT COUNTRY YOU
ARE IN, THE FRONT BRAKE LEVER IS ON THE RIGHT
OR SOMETIMES THE LEFT UNLESS THE BIKE IS SET UP
"MOTO STYLE."

THE PROBLEM WiTH MiTTENS

"HELLO." "F-OFF!"

CROSS COUNTRY RIDERS VS DOWNHILLERS

THE NEVER ENDING BATTLE BETWEEN THOSE WHO WANT TO
PEDAL UP THE HILL AND THOSE WHO WANT TO COAST DOWN IT.

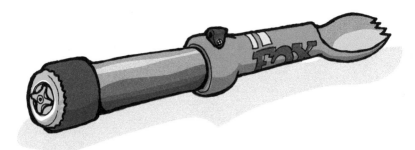

SUSPENSION SPORK

Full SUSPENSiON

GUACSHOX

BiKE PEDALS
EXPLAINED

FLAT PEDAL
NO CLiP THiNG
i.e. "CLiP-LESS"

CLiPLESS PEDAL
HAS CLiPPY THiNG THAT
CLiPS TO SHOE

BACK BEFORE THEY iNVENTED FLAT PEDALS

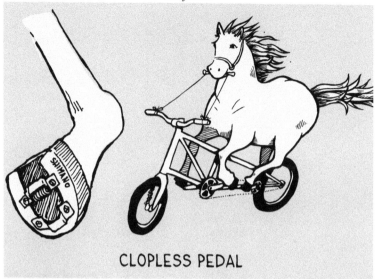

CLOPLESS PEDAL

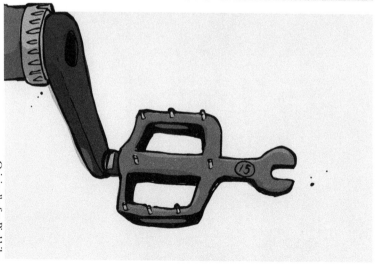

PEDAL WRENCH

PARKING LOT STYLE.

IF iT WAS SOCiALLY ACCEPTABLE TO WEAR THE REST OF
YOUR CLOTHES MASK-DANGLiNG-FROM-ONE-EAR
-iN-THE-PARKiNG-LOT STYLE.

POOR OL' TARZAN, HE ONLY HAD ONE iTEM OF CLOTHiNG TO WORRY ABOUT FOR MOST OF HiS LiFE, AND THEN THiNGS GOT COMPLiCATED.

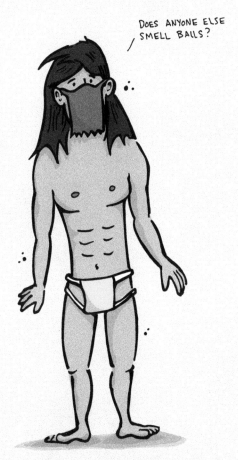

TARZAN GOT DRESSED iN THE DARK AGAiN.

7 SKATEBOARD TRICKS YOU PROBABLY SHOULDN'T DO

1. THESE.

2. BOARD SLIDE THIS RAIL.

3. THE ONE WHERE YOU LAND LIKE THIS.

4. FULL SPEED REVERSE HIPPIE JUMPS.

5. THIS GRIND.

6. STAIR GAPS WITH THIS PEBBLE AROUND.

7. THIS DOUBLES FREESTYLE TRICK.

MISO HORNET

EYE CONTACT AND THE MINI-PUMP

#FREE THE SPOKE NIPPLE

BELT DRIVE

I'M TRYING TO USE MY PHONE LESS.

PROBABLY SHOULDN'T DO THIS TO A FRIEND'S BIKE WITH A PAINT MARKER

Probably Shouldn't Do This to a Friend's Bike with a Paint Marker

WHY? BECAUSE IT'S BETTER FOR YOU THAN GFFEE

I'M ABOUT TO. —

IS ROCKY MOUNTAIN THIS BIKE?

MANUAL TRAINER

SUPERMAN TRAINER

Originally for Pinkbike

WALLRiDE TRAiNER

HEEL-CLiCKER TRAiNER

117

Originally for Pinkbike

MY PETS WATCH ME ON MY ZWIFT TRAINER

My Pets Watch Me Zwift

Think up Cool Things and Make Them Real

As a kid, I was taught and told over and over to "use your imagination." I was usually given this instruction when I was complaining about being bored, or when I was dragged to some adult gathering that was actually boring. I grew up thinking of imagination as entertainment. Maybe in the same way kids today get handed an iPad loaded with movies when they are bored, I was reminded to retreat into my mind and wander around the stories that were playing inside my head.

The adults either didn't know or didn't get across the crucial next step of imagination: If you think up something really cool, something you really want to actually exist, **you can make it happen**. It will take some work (maybe a lifetime of work) but you can make it real.

Dreaming up things is great, and honing that skill so you're able to envision new things is precious. Valuing the work it takes to learn the skills that can bring your idea alive are too often left out of the equation. I've spent a lot of the latter half of my life learning skills I wished I'd learned as a kid. Learning new things can be a lot more work than lazing around on the couch imagining them, but seeing a project in real life, in the real world, is more than worth the effort.

4 FAILED DESIGNS FROM THE PROTOTYPE LAB

1. "WIDE HANDLEBARS ARE POPULAR IN MOUNTAIN BIKING, BUT WHAT ABOUT WIDE BOTTOM BRACKETS?"

2. "A LOWER CENTER OF GRAVITY MIGHT BE HELPFUL."

3. "WE'VE TRIED ERGONOMIC BIKE DESIGNS, WHAT IF WE WENT THE OTHER DIRECTION?"

4. "CUSTOMERS ARE COMPLAINING THAT SITTING ON A BIKE SEAT IS UNCOMFORTABLE."

Originally for Pinkbike

PEE FREE...

SO MANY WAYS TO GO.

THE LONG HAUL TRUCKER
AT A TRUCK STOP IN IOWA

THE SHOWER

THE ROAD TRIP

THE TOUR DE FRANCE

THE BAD ETIQUETTE

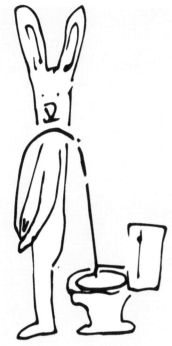

THE OVER-THE-SHOULDER   THE REALLY BAD ETIQUETTE

THE TOO TIRED TO GET
OUT OF BED BANKSHOT

THE TURN THE LIGHT OFF
FROM BED

129

THE OPEN THE PUBLIC
BATHROOM DOOR WITHOUT
TOUCHING THE HANDLE WITH
FRESHLY WASHED HANDS

THE PICKING A FLOOR
ON AN ELEVATOR WITH
YOUR HANDS FULL OF
GROCERIES

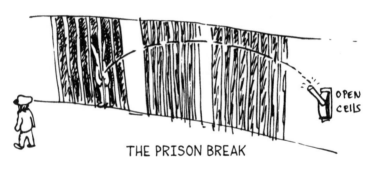

THE PRISON BREAK

THE CROWD CONTROL
(AKA THE CORRIGAN)

THE CLEAR THE CAT OFF THE
THANKSGIVING DINNER TABLE

THE PUSH BUTTON ENGINE START

THE NO SMOKING ON
THE SUBWAY

THE DON'T WRITE CHECKS
IN THE EXPRESS LANE

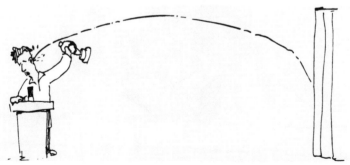

THE TIME TO WRAP UP THE SPEECH AT THE AWARDS SHOW

IT WOULD SUCK TO BE A BEDWETTING BAT

8 MORE BMX TRICKS YOU PROBABLY SHOULDN'T DO.

1. NO HANDED SUPERMAN WITH YOUR TONGUE IN THE PIVOTAL® SLIT.

2. THREADING YOUR HANDLEBARS THROUGH YOUR STRETCHED EAR LOBES.

3. TRIPLE BARSPIN WITHOUT TAKING YOUR HANDS OFF YOUR GRIPS.

4. DOING THIS DOWN A STAIR GAP.

5. PUTTING YOUR SEAT REALLY HIGH SO YOU CAN DO POLE DANCING MOVES.

6. LANDING LIKE THIS.

7. WHATEVER THIS NOSE MANUAL IS.

8. BLINDFOLDED PEDAL KICK FLIPS WITH 80's BMX RACING PEDALS.

12 YOGA Poses

The Broken Lock Pose

Find peace while using a public restroom.

②

Chin Hair Scratches Chest Pose

"...or is my chest hair scratching my chin?"

Feel the Wind From the Next Mat Over Pose

"Sally! WTF?
Did you eat a burning tire?!"

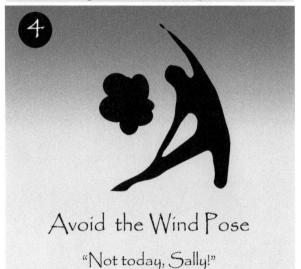

Avoid the Wind Pose

"Not today, Sally!"

Dropped My Danged Milkshake on the Floor

"Oh, but look, some splattered onto my shin and I can lick it off."

Complete Disbelief Pose

"You used all my oatmilk?!?"

7

Tryin' to Walk Up These Big Ol' Stairs Pose

"Why the fuck are these stairs so f-in' big?"

8

Everyone's New Year's Resolution was to Go to Yoga Pose

Classes are a bit too full for comfort for a few weeks.

Is it Worms?

"Don't tell me... I don't want to know."

Put a Grape in My Belly Button and I Can Launch it Into My Mouth

"And Mom says my college years were wasted."

Why They Only Give You Slip-On Shoes Pose

"Help, I got my fingers tangled in my shoe laces again!"

A Stupid Way to Clap

Just clap like a normal person, weirdo.

8 THINGS YOU PROBABLY SHOULDN'T DO AT THE GYM

1. THIS EXERCISE.

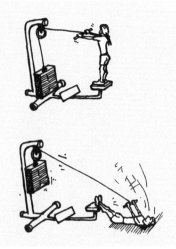

2. THIS EXERCISE TOO.

3. THIS WITH A BONER.

4. MIX UP THE SAND FILLED SLAM BALL WITH THE BOUNCY MEDICINE BALL (I DID THIS).

5. THE RUSTY CABLE CROSS.

6. LAY ALL YOUR WEIGHT ACROSS THE CONTROL PANEL OF THE TREADMILL AND JUST KIND OF DRAG YOUR FEET.

7. GET A QUICK BRAZILIAN WHILE USING THIS MACHINE.

8. DUCT TAPE YOUR FEET TO THE YOGA BALLS, GRAB THE FOAM ROLLERS, AND DECLARE WAR!

WHICH CAME FIRST?

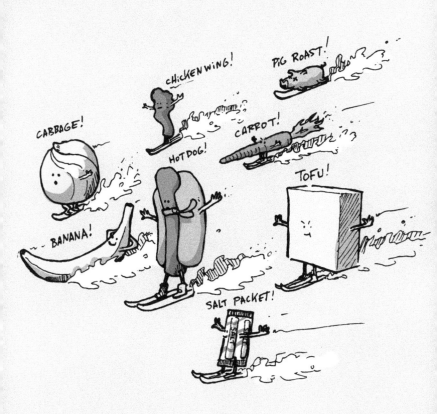

FAST FOOD.

PUGS NOT DRUGS.

CHAIN SMOKING ON THE TRAIL IS GROSS.

HUMANS:
USE YOUR WATER BOTTLE TO KEEP FERAL DOGS AWAY.

FERAL DOGS:
LURE HUMANS CLOSE BY WAGGING TAIL.

Originally for Fairdale Bikes

ME WHEN I CONVINCE THE BIKE SHOP TO LET ME USE
THEIR TOOLS TO SET UP A TUBELESS TIRE.

8 THINGS THAT PROBABLY SUCK
ABOUT BEING A UNICORN

1. YOU'LL NEVER OUTDO LAST YEAR'S
HELICOPTER COSTUME.

2. NO ONE TAKES YOUR DEATH METAL BAND SERIOUSLY.

3. EVERYONE KNOWS IT WAS YOU WHO CLOGGED UP
THE TOILET AT THE OFFICE.

4. YOU LOOK LIKE A TELETUBBY IN A HOODIE AND
RACIST IN A GHOST COSTUME.

5. HOW DO YOU PUT THIS DOWN?

6. GETTING BEAT UP AT THE GYM FOR PUTTING YOUR SOCK ON.

7. WIZARDS BE CREEPIN'.

8. EVEN WHEN IT IS REALLY SUNNY, YOU STILL HAVE TO WEAR YOUR BASEBALL HAT BACKWARDS.

Creativity Comes In Waves

Creativity comes in waves. That's not to say you can just sit back and wait for the tide to roll in—you have to make the waves yourself.

The death of creativity is staring at a blank page trying to figure out what you want to create. A blank page is perfectly still water. Nothing moving and nothing happening.

You are staring at that blank page because there is something inside you. That you don't yet fully comprehend or even understand what it might be is just fine. You can't create something before you've created it!

Start. Start scribbling, start typing... those first scratches act as the first ripples across the blank page's pool. It might not feel like you are making any progress, but if you keep at it, those tiny ripples build and amplify.

Good ideas will challenge you. Who do you think you are, dragging them into the light of day from their comfortable home floating through the intangible world of the creative ether? If you want to share them with the rest of us, it is going to take some work.

Work it, churn up momentum. Grow the waves.

Stay
Motivated

CPSIA information can be obtained
at www.ICGtesting.com
Printed in the USA
BVHW021805231120
594021BV00017B/244